CW01021004

Contents

How to pass the Trinity CertTESOL

Introduction

This publication contains information about passing the Trinity CertTESOL course, starting from your first contact with a course provider to getting your CertTESOL certificate.

This publication is written by EBC Servicios Lingüísticos Europe SL. EBC is a Trinity College London Validated Course Provider number 65747. Find out more about EBC at **https://ebcteflcourse.com**.

This publication contains some language learning and teaching technical terms. If you are not sure what these terms mean, please look at **Appendix B – Terminology and definitions**.

What is the Trinity CertTESOL?

If you have done your research, you already know that the Trinity CertTESOL is one of the best two accredited TESOL certificates in the world. If you have not, keep reading to find out more about the Trinity CertTESOL course and how to pass it.

Background

Trinity College London is one of **the world's largest educational organisations**. It examines almost one million people a year in over sixty countries.

Trinity TESOL qualifications are recognised globally by prominent employers as solid, quality controlled and professionally sound qualifications.

Trinity College London is the only examination board in the UK that provides examinations and higher vocational qualifications across many communicative arts.

The aims of a Trinity CertTESOL course

The technical definition of the **Trinity CertTESOL** course is that it is:

"a pre-service teacher training course at level 5 of the Regulated Qualifications Framework (RQF)"

It is a course to train people to teach English, and the course's academic level is the same as years 1 and 2 at university.

The **Trinity CertTESOL** trains you in the foundation skills and knowledge you need to get a job as an ESOL teacher. It also gives you confidence and a solid base for self-evaluation and professional development.

The **Trinity CertTESOL** is for people who have little or no experience teaching English to speakers of other languages (TESOL) and teaching English as a foreign language (TEFL).

Special note for non-native English speakers

Trinity CertTESOL trainees must have a high level of spoken and written English. English does not have to be the trainee's first language. However, English as a second language speakers must have a good enough English level to enter an English-speaking university. Acceptable scores are at least an IELTS 6.5, TOEFL iBT 80 or anything else equivalent to the **Common European Framework of Reference for Languages** C1 level.

The objectives of a Trinity CertTESOL course

By the time you finish the Trinity CertTESOL course, you must show that you have achieved the following:

- Have a working knowledge of the main grammatical, lexical and phonological features of English
- Are aware of the learning needs of individual learners and groups of learners
- Understand learner motivation in different cultures and contexts
- Know how to establish rapport and create and maintain learner interest
- Know how to write lesson plans with clear and achievable aims, using appropriate methods for different learner levels
- Know how to manage and stimulate active participation among a group of learners
- Create a learning environment and learning opportunities aligned to learning objectives
- Know how to evaluate, create, use and adapt teaching material
- Understand the pros and cons of mainstream language teaching approaches
- Be able to assess your effectiveness as a teacher and work as a member of a teaching team
- Understand how to continue your development as an English teacher
- Understand how to get an English teaching job after passing the course
- Understand the main issues relevant to employment as an English teacher

So how do you learn all this stuff?

The Trinity CertTESOL course structure and its units

The **Trinity CertTESOL** course has five units broken down as follows:

Unit	Hours	Details
Unit 1: Teaching Skills	74	This Unit covers: • methodology, • teaching skills, • teaching practice, • guided observation, • coursebook and materials evaluation, • methods of assessment and testing in the classroom. This is the largest Unit. It involves assessing your teaching skills, knowledge and understanding. You must demonstrate these areas in your written work, teaching practice and during your one-on-one interview with the independent external moderator. The Trinity CertTESOL prepares you specifically for the initial stages of teaching English, so there are more guided learning hours in Unit 1 than in the other four units. In addition, Unit 1 makes sure that the quality, validity, relevance and professional integrity of the Trinity CertTESOL stick to Ofqual and international standards.
Unit 2: Language Awareness & Skills	20	This Unit teaches you essential theoretical knowledge of English linguistic form (phonology, lexis and syntax), function and meaning. Unit 2 also shows you how to teach this knowledge to your ELLs. You must pass tests to pass Unit 2.
Unit 3: Learner Profile	18	This Unit covers one-to-one teaching methodology, needs analysis, linguistic analysis, lesson planning and syllabus design. In the form of a practical assignment, it brings together all the items you learned in Units 1 and 2.

Unit	Hours	Details
Unit 4: The Materials Assignment	8	This Unit covers the production, adaptation, use and evaluation of simple classroom teaching materials and concept checking tasks. You will use the teaching materials you produce in your teaching practice lessons. An independent external moderator assesses your Unit 4 work and decides whether you passed or failed Unit 4.
Unit 5: Unknown Language	10	This Unit covers teaching methodologies and activities appropriate for beginner-level language learners with little or no use of their first language (L1). You and your classmates are language learners, so you get to experience what it is like to be a beginner level language learner. It also introduces you to lesson planning and contrastive analysis, where you compare aspects of the unknown language to English. FYI, the foreign languages we use for your unknown language classes could be Polish, Norwegian, Hebrew and Tagalog.

The Trinity CertTESOL timetable

The minimum course length is 130 timetabled hours plus 70 non-timetabled hours, a total qualification time of 200 hours.

Timetabled hours

Allocated time	Timeslot content
90 hours of supervised input which can be in the form of online study and trainer input	• group work and tutorials • input sessions for course components • teaching practice feedback • supervised workshops • supervised lesson planning • initial planning session to prepare interviews for the Learner Profile • initial planning session for the Materials Assignment • tests/exams

	• group and individual interviews with the independent external moderator (mandatory)
10 hours of teaching and observation	• a minimum of six hours of observed and assessed teaching practice (mandatory) • a minimum of four hours of guided observation of classes given by experienced teachers (live or recorded) with English language learners (mandatory)
30 hours for assignment preparation and completion	• preparation for teaching and completion of your Unit 1 - Teaching Practice Portfolio • Preparation for your Unit 2 – Language Awareness test • preparation and completion of your Unit 3 - Learner Profile Journal • preparation for your Unit 4 - Materials Assignment Journal • preparation and completion of your Unit 5 - Unknown Language Journal
70 hours non-timetabled hours for	• reading, research, assignment writing, lesson planning and preparation.

The Trinity CertTESOL course is solid, structured and unique

One of the world's largest educational organisations backs the **Trinity CertTESOL**, so you know it is solid and reliable.

This publication introduces you to the structure that is the backbone of the **Trinity CertTESOL** course. It is a tried and tested structure that is world-famous because it thoroughly prepares you to start teaching English as a foreign language.

The Trinity CertTESOL course is unique

The **Trinity CertTESOL** has one competitor called CELTA. Our competitor's study programme has some similarities, but the primary focus is different. Here is an article if you would like to know **what is the difference between the Trinity CertTESOL and CELTA**.

The **Trinity CertTESOL** helps you find your "inner teacher", which may sound a bit hippy, but I don't know how else to describe it. The **Trinity CertTESOL** gives you a structured set of tools that you use and adapt to who you are, how you think and how you teach. So you constantly think, assess and re-assess what you are doing and where you are going as a teacher. This self-reflection is invaluable because it is the key to your growth and improvement as an English teacher. In comparison, the CELTA tells you how to teach, and you have to follow their playbook.

We also know that loads of other companies are trying to take your money for their own TEFL certificates. Many will say and do anything (including deception tactics) to convince you that their certificate is internationally accepted and will help you get a teaching job.

Do not be fooled by these companies! There are no TEFL qualifications directly equivalent to the **Trinity CertTESOL** and the CELTA.

The six phases to pass the Trinity CertTESOL

Here are the six steps to passing the Trinity CertTESOL. More detail about these steps appear later in this publication.

The six steps are

1. Applying for the Trinity CertTESOL course
2. Pre-admission interview written assignment
3. The admission interview
4. Pre-course preparation after acceptance
5. Passing your course units
6. Passing your external moderation

When you complete the six steps, you get your Trinity CertTESOL certificate.

Step 1 - Applying for the Trinity CertTESOL course

Your first step to passing the Trinity CertTESOL is to apply to take the course.

Applying for a course usually means filling out an application form and sending it to the course provider.

Here is a sample list of the type of information you submit when you apply for a Trinity CertTESOL course.

1. Your first and last name
2. Your birth year
3. Your nationality
4. Your mother tongue (aka first language or L1)
5. Your educational qualifications
6. Why you want to take the course
7. State if you have any educational or physical special needs for your training

To move to step 2, the **pre-admission interview written assignment**, you must meet Trinity College London's three minimum entry requirements. If you do not meet these three minimum entry requirements, you will not start the admission process.

1. You must be at least 18 years old on the first day of the course.
2. You must show that you have qualifications for entry to higher education (college or university level) in your home country.
3. You must have a high level of English language competence (reading, writing, speaking, listening) appropriate for an English teacher and good enough to understand the course material and assignments. If English is not your first language, you should have an English level of C1 on the

Common European Framework of Reference (CEFR) in all four skills. In addition, you must demonstrate an acceptable English level throughout the initial written assessment and admissions interview.

If you meet these three Trinity College London requirements, your application moves to the next step.

Equal opportunity

All Trinity College London validated course providers must have an equal opportunities statement. Here is EBC's as an example of what an equal opportunity statement could look like.

> *EBC accepts and enrols students continuously during the year. The admissions staff treat each application carefully, evaluate personal and intellectual qualities, and make every effort to be thorough, sensitive, and fair.*
>
> *Our goal is to bring together groups with high academic ability, professional experience, and various backgrounds, particular interests, accomplishments, and aspirations. EBC offers a course where students have much to offer and learn from each other.*

The purpose of this is to prevent discrimination based on gender, sex, marital status, race, colour, religion, disability, age, language, social origin and other sensitive personal such as political opinions, sexual preferences and non-binary gender preferences.

Step 2- Pre-admission interview written assignment

Trinity College London requires that everyone who is accepted to take a Trinity CertTESOL completes a handwritten assignment.

There is no fixed topic or number of words for the written assignment. However, 200 to 300 words are acceptable. The topic depends on the course provider's choice, but is usually something like "What do you think are the qualities of a successful language teacher and why you should be admitted?".

The purpose of the handwritten assignment is to make sure that you can write using a pen without having something like **Grammarly** giving you corrective tips. You will not have **Grammarly** in a classroom, and at some time during your teaching career, you will need to write by hand. Note that some cultures interpret inadequate or inaccurate handwriting as a sign of illiteracy.

This assignment checks that you write with a reasonable degree of accuracy.

A special note for non-native English speakers

Your Trinity CertTESOL course provider bases part of your acceptance on the written assignment. At the end of the course, you can be failed by Trinity College if the independent external moderator decides that your standard of English is significantly below that required for an English teacher. For this reason, we strongly recommend that you take the handwritten test very seriously and do not cheat or get someone else to write it for you.

Step 3 - The admission interview

The admission interview must demonstrate that you will be a good fit and cope with course expectations. If you are a non-native English speaker, the interview also checks that your English knowledge is satisfactory for taking the course.

You must pass the admission interview to get offered a course place

---

Trinity College does not have a set of specific admission interview questions. Instead, Trinity College defines what must be checked during the admission interview. The pre-admission interview reviews the following:

- You can work cooperatively as a member of your training group
- You will respond constructively to feedback on personal performance
- You can work under pressure because the training is rigorous and demands time, energy and emotional stamina
- You must disclose any educational or physical special needs
- If the course you attend includes teaching practice with minors, you are asked if you have a criminal record
- You need to show a photo ID to confirm your identity

Here is an example of a set of admission interview questions.

1. What is your work and educational background?
2. What do you hope to get from the course?
3. Are you interested in restricting yourself to an age group or a teaching discipline?
4. What do you think are the qualities of a successful language teacher?
5. What personal qualities would you bring to the classroom?
6. The CertTESOL course is intensive.
    a. Have you got any outside obligations?
    b. How will you cope with the workload?
    c. Do you have family commitments?
7. In many of the input sessions / TP feedback, it will be necessary to work closely with classmates.
    a. How do you feel about this?
    b. Can you work in a team?
8. If you have any educational or physical special needs for your training, what are they?
9. If you have a criminal record, what is it?

The admission interview result

You get informed, usually within two working days, whether or not you passed the admission interview. If you pass the admission interview, you move to the next step. If not, you are informed of what you need to improve to get accepted. If you make the improvements, you are welcome to apply again.

Step 4 -Pre-course preparation after acceptance

You are informed of your course acceptance.

Enrolment payment

The Trinity CertTESOL is one of the two best TEFL certificates in the world and is in high demand. Therefore, almost all Trinity College London validated course providers will ask for a course deposit to enrol and guarantee your course place.

Course providers ask for a deposit to ensure that they send the Trinity College required pre-course preparation pack to enrolled trainees. If someone has not enrolled, why send pre-course preparation work?

After you pay for the Trinity CertTESOL course, you are sent a course handbook or **Welcome Pack**. You will receive your **Welcome Pack** no later than the day before your classes start. Most course providers send the **Welcome Pack** in advance of the course start date. At a minimum, your **Welcome Pack** will contain or refer to the following:

1. Details of the course provider
2. Details of Trinity's CertTESOL qualification
3. Details of course tutors and administrators
4. Local details (e.g. course access, facilities, resource access, etc.)
5. Details of course assignments
6. Details of progress assessment
7. Your responsibilities as a trainee
8. Emergency procedures and contact numbers
9. A copy of the course timetable and a list of assignment deadlines

Pre-course work

In addition, some course providers (EBC is one of them) will send you pre-course preparation material about teaching and grammar. If your course provider sends you this additional material, we recommend reading it because it helps.

If you do not get extra teaching and grammar material from your course provider, we recommend that you look for and read this type of material.

Getting ready to study

The Trinity CertTESOL is a demanding course. The estimated number of hours to complete the course is around 200 over four weeks. Doing the maths, that's 50 hours a week.

You must ensure that you do not have any time-consuming personal commitments while you are taking the course.

If you are taking the course online or there is an online component:

1. make sure that you have a distraction-free location to do your coursework
2. do coursework on a computer rather than on a tablet or smartphone
3. make sure that you have a reliable internet connection

4. take a 5-minute break every hour when doing computer-based reading or exercises
5. use a comfortable chair when you use the computer

Preparing and committing yourself to the course are essential if you want to pass.

Step 5 - Passing your course units

To understand how you pass the Trinity CertTESOL, you need to know how you get assessed. The more you understand what the assessment is looking for, the better you can do your assignments and pass all five Units.

Grades

The Trinity CertTESOL course has two grades:

1. Pass
2. Referral

Pass is self-explanatory.

Referral means that you failed one or more course Units (usually Unit 4); however, you are allowed to retake the Unit. If you retake the referred Unit(s) and pass, you pass the course and get your Trinity CertTESOL. The purpose of **Referral** is to give you a second chance and not write you off as a failure. Having said this, it is a lot better if you pass the first time around.

Assignments

Units 1, 3, 4 and 5 have written journals, and Unit 2 has a timed test under examination conditions. Each Unit is discussed in detail later in this publication.

An independent external moderator visits your course at the end of your course. The independent external moderator will spot-check your written assignments and give you your grade for **Unit 4 – Materials assignment**.

Your written work must be quality. The independent external moderator will see your level of written English, and the independent external moderator will talk to you. The independent external moderator can fail you if your English is weak.

In addition to written work, you will teach six one-hour English lessons to groups of English language learners (ELLs). One or more of the course trainers will observe each lesson and give you feedback. Your classmates will also watch two of your classes as part of the Unit 1 work.

Basic pass criteria

You pass the CertTESOL course when you complete all the coursework to the required standard, and you can demonstrate:

1. basic knowledge of English grammar, form, function and phonology for teaching
2. knowledge of the fundamental issues relating to language learning and teaching
3. an understanding of the importance of your ELLs' academic and emotional needs

4. able to make teaching material and lesson plans for different learner levels
5. able to use standard classroom aids
6. competence in teaching and evaluating EFL classes
7. an awareness of how to use reference materials and professional guidance to increase your language and teaching skills
8. a capability of teamwork in a creative and critical setting
9. an ability to provide coursework to the level of English expected of an English teacher
10. an ability to deliver coursework on time and in line with coursework expectations

Assessment criteria

Overall pass or fail assessment is based on performance in the following areas:

- The quality of your Unit 1, 3, 4 and 5 written work
- The result of your Unit 2 test
- The result of your Unit 4 interview with the independent external moderator
- The quality of your six observed teaching practice classes
- Your overall behaviour (interaction, contribution, teamwork, enthusiasm)
- The quality of your lesson preparation (innovation, planning, material usage, time management)
- Your teaching practice lesson delivery (style, interaction, dynamism, progress checking)
- Your general approach to the course, your peers, trainer(s), teaching practice students, and other associated people (delivering your assignments on time, punctuality, courteous behaviour, team-oriented, appropriately dressed)

Your course provider will give you further details about how you get assessed in the **Welcome Pack** you received.

Assignment delivery deadlines

Your **Welcome Pack** should tell you when you have to deliver your assignments. In addition, you usually get a detailed course timetable and your teaching practice schedule on the first day of the course.

Written assignments must demonstrate a grammar, spelling, and punctuation level in line with an English teacher's skills.

Tutorials and trainer feedback

Your trainer continuously assesses your assignments and progress throughout the course and gives you feedback. If you get asked to take action resulting from the feedback, you must do it or risk failing the course. If your trainer thinks that you may not pass the course, you will get a clear warning of the lack of progress verbally and in writing. In addition, you get an action plan for remedial work with concrete target dates. If you do not deliver the remedial work on time, you may fail the course.

Resource citations

Some units require you to provide references to external resources. When you use external resource material, you must provide a bibliography citing your sources. The recommended citation style is **Harvard Citation**. Ask your centre which citation style they expect.

A basic **Harvard Citation** contains the author, title of the publication, publisher and source.

Here is an example:

Author	Usma, F.
Title	"Approaches and Methods in Language Teaching - Approaches and Methods in Language Teaching, Second Edition"
Publisher	www.academia.edu. [online]
Source	https://www.academia.edu/9863136/Approaches_and_Methods_in_Language _Teaching_Approaches_and_Methods_in_Language_Teaching_Second_Edit ion

Plagiarism

Plagiarism is using someone else's words and ideas as if they were yours without acknowledging their source. You will automatically fail the course if you plagiarise material. You may use other people's material, but you must indicate the source using your course provider's citation protocol.

Unit 1 – Teaching skills

Unit content

1. An overview of the primary methodologies and theories of English language learning, language acquisition, and English Language Learner (ELL) needs
2. Lesson planning using different styles and methods
3. Combining methodology, approach and lesson planning to teach the four skills: reading, writing, speaking and listening
4. English language grammatical, lexical and phonological components
5. Assessing ELL needs to enable effective lesson planning and remedial activities
6. Analysing mistakes and creating corrective solutions
7. Selecting suitable teaching materials for the taught skill, e.g. visuals for explaining emotions, audio for listening skills, etc.
8. Developing simple teaching material to meet specific learner aims
9. Self-evaluation and evaluation by your trainer(s)
10. An overview of the leading public exams in ESOL
11. The primary forms of English language testing

What you must achieve

Upon successful completion of Unit 1, you should:

1. Understand how to use TESOL approaches, methodologies and classroom management skills that match your teaching aims and your ELL's backgrounds and learning objectives
2. Be able to competently use materials and teaching aids with imagination and an awareness of how they support learning requirements
3. Be aware of the critical features of presentation, form, function and relevance to your ELLs as set out in coursebooks and materials
4. The ability to assess your strengths and weaknesses to identify your further training needs and to evaluate your classmates comparatively

Lesson planning

You must be able to:

1. Determine what you want to achieve in the lesson and how you get there
2. Identify your ELLs' learning needs and preferences
3. Understand how to motivate your ELLs
4. Use, adopt and adapt different teaching methods and styles for diverse ELLs
5. Use a learner-centred approach in lesson planning
6. Balance accuracy (correcting mistakes) with fluency (letting the conversation flow) as teaching aims

Lesson execution

You must be able to:

1. Use techniques that encourage confidence, creativity and cooperation in your ELLs

2. Strike a balance between teacher (you) to ELL and ELL to ELL involvement
3. Give clear instructions and explanations and ensure your ELLs understood
4. Manage error correction in a tactful and constructive way
5. Establish and maintain rapport with your ELLs
6. Organise and manage your classroom
7. Manage class activity, pair work, group work and individual work
8. Use teaching aids and materials that achieve your aim
9. Adapt and use teaching materials effectively
10. Use authentic and self-made teaching materials
11. Use a range of tasks and activities to achieve your aims and objectives

Post-lesson reflection

You must be able to:

1. Identify the lesson's aims and the learning objectives you did or did not achieve
2. Identify why you did or did not achieve the learning objectives
3. Note down adaptations of your approach or materials for future classes
4. Evaluate the effectiveness of the teaching material you used
5. Gauge the strengths and weaknesses of your lesson
6. Weigh up the feasibility of your lesson's aims
7. Prioritise the strengths you want to develop or weaknesses you want to strengthen in future lessons

You demonstrate and document these skills in:

1. Observed and assessed teaching practice classes
2. Your **Teaching Practice Portfolio**
3. Your **Guided Observation Journal**

These three elements are your **Unit 1 -Teaching skills** assignments.

Your course provider will give you templates to complete your **Unit 1 -Teaching skills** assignments. The content of these templates refer to the following:

Teaching practice portfolio

The portfolio contains the following:

1. Lesson plans for your observed and assessed teaching practice classes, in date order, referring to:
   a. ELL information (e.g. number of attendees, approximate ages, level, additional notes, etc.)
   b. English skill level of the class
   c. Lesson aims
   d. Progress expectation
   e. How you got to your lesson aim
   f. Lesson task and activity order and timing
   g. The teaching materials you used
   h. Potential problems you might encounter and how you will handle them

      i. How you will assess that your ELLs learned what you wanted them to know

2. A reflection of your performance for each lesson showing:
   a. What you did and did not achieve in the lesson?
   b. Why did you succeed or fail to achieve?
   c. What methods will you keep and adapt for future classes?
   d. Were your teaching materials effective?
   e. In hindsight, was your lesson aim feasible and/or realistic?
   f. What were the strengths and weaknesses of your lesson?
   g. What will you do to improve your teaching approach for your next lesson?
3. Your trainer assesses your lessons regarding:
   a. What you achieved and not achieved in the lesson
   b. What you succeeded and failed to achieve
   c. The methods should you keep and adapt for future classes
   d. The effectiveness of your teaching materials
   e. An assessment about the feasibility and realism of your lesson aim
   f. The strengths and weaknesses of your lesson
   g. What you should do to improve your teaching approach for your next lesson
4. The teaching materials you used in the lesson
5. A final summary where you:
   a. Reflect on your development as a teacher
   b. Describe your strengths as an English teacher
   c. Prioritise areas you want to improve and develop

Guided observation journal

Guided observation shows you teachers in action and lets you learn by seeing what they do and how they teach. You watch three or four one-hour classes taught by experienced teachers. You watch the first class before you teach your first class. The lessons you observe can be live or recorded.

Based on what you observe and discuss with your trainer(s) and classmates, you create your guided observation journal with one entry per observed class. Each entry contains:

1. The level of class and the type of ELLs attending the class
2. The lesson length
3. Aims of the lesson
4. Observation aims (the course provider gives you a list of things to look for in each class, e.g. describe the teacher's rapport with the class as a whole, comment on the teacher language, specifically when giving instructions and explanations)
5. Comments and observations about the teaching process and learning results

Peer observation journal

Peer observation gives you the chance to see how your classmates teach. You will watch at least two of your classmates teach, write up what you saw and include it in your journal.

Each entry contains:

1. The level of class and the type of ELLs attending the class
2. The lesson length
3. Aims of the lesson
4. Your classmate's rapport with the ELLs
5. Delivery style (e.g. talking speed, vocal clarity and volume, language use matched (or did not match) the ELLs' ability)
6. Comments and observations about the teaching process and learning results

Teaching practice

You will give six hours of observed and assessed teaching practice to ELLs. You will teach to at least two different ability levels. You should also get the chance to rehearse your classes with your trainer and classmates before giving the class. The rehearsals are not part of the six hours observed and assessed teaching practice classes.

You get your teaching practice schedule when you start the course. It shows the date, time, level, the trainer's name who will observe you, and your classmate's name who will observe you.

If you are teaching in a virtual classroom, make sure you know how to operate the software before teaching your class. Technical issues are not acceptable excuses, and they may mean that you fail the lesson and possibly fail the course.

Testing and assessment

You get guidance about the primary forms of formative and summative English language assessment. Testing and assessment measure performance in the four skills: reading, writing, listening and speaking.

1. Formative assessment measures ongoing progress and has feedback, e.g. a quiz about one of the course topics.
2. Summative assessment creates a final evaluation, usually with a grade, e.g. an examination for all course topics.

You will also be made aware of the Trinity College London ESOL exams:

1. Graded Examinations in Spoken English (**GESE**)
2. Integrated Skills in English (**ISE**).

You will get shown other test names as well.

You do not get a grade for testing and assessment. However, the independent external moderator will ask whether or not you learned about it, especially the Trinity tests.

Unit 2 – Language awareness

This Unit is about spelling, grammar, phonetics, pronunciation, etc.

By the time you finish this Unit and the rest of the course units, you should have achieved the following:

	What you need to learn	Where you get assessed
1.	Understand how English language form, function and meaning work together	Pre-course tasks Unit 1 - teaching practice **Unit 2 - Language awareness test** Unit 3 - Learner profile
2.	Awareness of concepts and terminology that describe English use and structure	Pre-course tasks Unit 1 - teaching practice **Unit 2 - Language awareness test**
3.	You can express your understanding of points 1. and 2. in terms of language skills and sub-skills	Unit 1 - lesson plan objectives Unit 3 - Learner profile
4.	Know how to teach English language form, function and meaning in a communicative classroom	Unit 1 - Teaching practice Unit 3 - Learner profile
5.	Understand how to combine form, function and meaning in a lesson plan or syllabus	Unit 1 - Teaching practice Unit 3 - Learner profile
6.	Know how to assess your ELLs' language skills	Unit 1 - Teaching practice Unit 3 - Learner profile
7.	Be aware of the various flavours of English around the world, the emergence of English as a lingua franca, and their teaching implications	Unit 1 - Teaching practice Unit 3 - Learner profile

	What you need to learn	Where you get assessed
8.	Be aware of how an ELL's language impacts the ELL's learning capability (interlingual interference)	Unit 1 - Teaching practice Unit 3 - Learner profile
9.	Be aware of current written and spoken language use, e.g. modern vocabulary, acceptable slang terms, gender-neutral notation, etc.	Unit 1 - Teaching practice Unit 3 - Learner profile Unit 5 - Unknown language completion of all training requirements, written and spoken
10.	Know how to find reference resources and how to research language teaching and skills	Pre-course tasks Unit 1 - Teaching practice Unit 3 - Learner profile

You study some of the technical aspects of English in your Trinity CertTESOL course. You learn through pre-course study tasks and timetabled input sessions.

The language awareness material covers lexis (vocabulary), grammar (structure) and phonology (sounds).

When you finish unit 2, you should be able to:

- research lexis, grammar and phonology from relevant sources
- apply your knowledge of lexis, grammar and phonology to:
  - Unit 1 Teaching skills
  - Unit 2 Language awareness
  - Unit 3 Learner profile
  - Unit 4 Materials assignment
  - Unit 4 Unknown language

Learning lexis and grammar

The following are covered:

1. Word classes and parts of speech for analysing language:
   a. Verbs: infinitive verbs, main verbs, auxiliary verbs, modal verbs, state verbs, action verbs, etc.
   b. Nouns, pronouns, countability

   c. Adjectives, adverbs, comparatives, superlatives
   d. Determiners with a focus on articles and quantifiers
   e. Conjunctions for coordinating and subordinating
   f. Prepositions
2. Syntactical elements for text and spoken analysis:
   a. Subject, predicate, objects (direct and indirect), adverbials and complements
   b. Phrases: noun, verb, prepositional, adverbial
3. Tenses:
   a. Tenses, form and time, inflexions, auxiliaries, modals, affirmative, negative and interrogative
   b. Active voice
   c. Passive voice
   d. Reported speech
4. Word formation and lexical relationships, for example:
   a. Derivation (creating new words using a prefix or suffix)
   b. Collocation (combined word phrases, e.g. get a job, throw a party, etc.)
   c. Synonyms (words with the same meaning)
   d. Hyponyms (subcategories of words, e.g. chair and table are both hyponyms of furniture)
   e. Phrasal verbs, e.g. to take off, to get up, to put down
5. Features of speech analysis:
   a. Understanding coherence and cohesion
   b. Punctuation and creating paragraphs
   c. The characteristics of spoken and written English
6. Language variation:
   a. Register: the level and style of English use in a given situation, e.g. "Hello" (formal), "Hi" (informal).
   b. Grammar and vocabulary variations between spoken and written language
   c. Geographical versions of English
7. Interlingual interference:
   a. How ELLs' first language can affect their English learning abilities

Learning phonology

The following are covered:

Content	Where you get assessed
1. Phonics (sounds) • Phonemic symbols – the International Phonetic Alphabet (IPA) • Consonants • Vowels • Diphthongs	Use and evaluation of techniques for teaching listening, speaking, and correcting errors, e.g.: • Articulation of phonemes • Using phonemic symbols and the IPA to describe and discriminate sounds

Content	Where you get assessed
• How sound and spelling are linked	• Transcribing speech • Visual stimuli, e.g. mime, showing fingers, pointing, object placement, gestures • Modelling techniques, e.g. choral, drilling, concatenation • Exercises to identifying individual sounds, e.g. minimal pairs • Indicating stress points and intonation in writing and using gestures • Combining speech (phonology) with vocabulary and grammar teaching • Teaching phonology to an individual ELL
2. Words and phrases • Word stress (weak and strong) • Contractions • Connected speech • Spoken sound flow	
3. Sentences and discourse • Word or phrase stress • Intonation	
4. General • Awareness of grammar • Phonology links • Contrastive analysis for diagnosing and correcting pronunciation errors • Analysing ELL difficulties in hearing and understanding spoken English • Analysing your pronunciation difficulties in the unknown language lessons • English as a method of global communication (English as a Lingua Franca aka ELF)	

Learning language skills

Language skills is a generic term for:

1. Receptive skills = listening and reading
2. Productive skills = speaking and writing

You will learn:

1. Different skills and sub-skills that support language learning
2. How to apply these skills for communicative learning and teaching
3. How to reflect on and evaluate their success

Listening sub-skills

1. Predicting outcomes, results, consequences, etc.
2. Gist identification
3. Find specific information, e.g. What day did the accident happen?
4. Cope with intensive and extensive activities
5. Deduction, e.g. What do you think "out in the cold" means?
6. Decoding (understanding speech rather than just hearing it)
7. Understand grammar structures, e.g. tense, modality, etc.
8. Understand syntax structures and relationships
9. Separate language form from language function (presentation versus use)
10. Spot cohesive devices (referring back to something, e.g. "This is a car. It is red." "It" refers to the car
11. Spot discourse markers (get attention, hesitate, interject, affirm) "Okay, here we are again." "Okay" is a discourse marker
12. Isolate the main points
13. Inferring

Reading sub-skills

1. Predicting outcomes, results, consequences, etc.
2. Spot the written style based on format and layout
3. Find things through titles, subtitles, indices, etc.
4. Skimming for meaning
5. Scanning for specific information
6. Cope with intensive and extensive activities
7. Deduction, e.g. What do you think "out in the cold" means?
8. Decoding (understanding the text rather than just reading the words)
9. Understand grammar structures, e.g. tense, modality, etc.
10. Understand syntax structures and relationships
11. Separate language form from language function (presentation versus use)
12. Spot cohesive devices (referring back to something, e.g. "This is a car. It is red." "It" refers to the car
13. Spot discourse markers (get attention, hesitate, interject, affirm) "Okay, here we are again." "Okay" is a discourse marker
14. Isolate the main points
15. Inferring

Speaking sub-skills

1. Saying phonemes and connected speech
2. Correctly stressing words and sentences
3. Correct use of intonation
4. Accurately grammar use
5. Accurate syntax use
6. Proper use of vocabulary, phrases and sentences to communicate ideas

7. Good use of cohesive devices, e.g. it, they, etc.
8. Accurate discourse marker use
9. Adjusting within the formal and informal range
10. Aligned body language and other non-verbal devices

Writing sub-skills

1. Accurate penmanship
2. Accurate spelling and punctuation
3. Correct grammar use
4. Accurate syntax use
5. Proper use of vocabulary, phrases and sentences to communicate ideas
6. Good use of cohesive devices, e.g. it, they, etc.
7. Accurate discourse marker use
8. Adjusting within the formal and informal range
9. Logical information flow
10. Matching the writing tone to the required style or mood
11. Writing drafts
12. Editing texts

Language tests

You take a language test that will ask questions based on Unit 2 content. You must pass the test to pass Unit 2. Each centre sets the passing grade, which is usually 60%.

Trinity does not have a standard set of questions. However, here are some examples of the areas that could be covered in your test.

These section examples are from the EBC Unit 2 test. The EBC test has 82 questions. You get 90 minutes to complete the test under exam conditions.

Word categorisation

Categorise words according to parts of speech

Word	Noun	Pronoun	Adjective	Adverb	Verb	Linking device
friendly			✓			

Find parts of English in a text

Read a text and find an example of each grammatical item in a list, e.g. find a conjunction.

Verb tenses

Write sentences to confirm with a list of different verb tenses, e.g. the negative form of the future perfect

Tenses relating to time

Draw a timeline to reflect a set of statements, e.g. By the time we arrived, the party had started.

Error identification and correction

Identify sentence errors and

1. write what the most likely correct version is
2. analyse the error using appropriate terminology
3. offer a possible reason for the error

Word pairs

Explain the difference between the commonly confused pairs of words, e.g. raise and rise.

Marking work

Identify the errors in a text by underlining and putting the appropriate code above the mistake.

Code

T	wrong tense	WO	word order	sp	spelling mistake
WW	wrong word	^	missing word	N	number, i.e. singular/plural
P	punctuation error	/	unnecessary word	A	wrong/missing article
		prep	incorrect preposition	R	wrong register

Explaining language structures

Create a brief context that exemplifies the use of the underlined structure. Then, note down two concept checking questions that you could ask students to determine their understanding of it.

Example: "I **have worked** here for seven years."

"Seven years ago, I was unemployed. Then I saw a job advertisement and applied. They gave me an interview. It went well, and I got the job! I worked hard and made some good friends. I now earn a decent amount of money, and I don't want to leave."

Concept checking question 1 – "Did I start work here seven years ago?"

Concept checking question 2 – "Do I still work here now?"

Phonetics

Fit the phonetic version of the word into the appropriate sentence, e.g.

Alice fought with her friend, and they had a /raʊ/ (row).

We stood in a /rəʊ/ (row).

/rəʊ/

/raʊ/

Unit 3 – Learner profile

This Unit is about analysing the needs of an ELL, creating a lesson, teaching the ELL, analysing the results and creating a programme of further study for the ELL.

By the time you finish this Unit and the rest of the course units, you should have achieved the following:

1. Written a simple linguistic profile and needs analysis for one ELL based on:
   a. a total of 60 to 90 minutes of one or more interviews with the ELL
   b. a sample of the ELL's written work and any tests you gave
   c. your interview notes must include a general discussion of the ELL's learning background, learning desires, preferred learning style, and any strengths and weaknesses you observed
2. Prepared and taught a 45 to 60-minute lesson. The lesson is not observed, and it is not part of your six hours of observed teaching practice.
3. Written a list of recommendations for the ELL's study programme in at least one area of each of the four primary skills. Your recommendations must include grammar and phonology.

Learner profile portfolio

Your portfolio contains:

1. A description of your ELL's cultural and social background, including language learning experience, when and where your ELL uses English, the reasons your ELL wants to learn English, when your ELL may use English in the future and the main linguistic features of the learner's mother tongue
2. An evaluation of your ELL's linguistic proficiency, including strengths and weaknesses in the four skills. Your analysis must look at lexis, grammar and phonology, and refer to relevant features of the learner's mother tongue. To perform this evaluation, you should:
   a. Record the ELL speaking English. **NOTE**: Keep the recording. You will need it to complete your Unit 3 work. In addition, the independent external moderator may ask to listen to it when you have your one-on-one moderation interview.
   b. Write down part of what the ELL said using standard English (orthographic transcription)
   c. Write down part of what the ELL said using the International Phonetic Alphabet (phonemic transcription)
   d. Get the ELL to write something in English that you can analyse for errors
   e. Give the ELL extensive and intensive listening and reading exercises
   f. Note down how the ELL interacts with you during the interview to get an idea of his/her interaction skills
3. A one-on-one lesson plan with a rationale and an evaluation based on selected key learning needs identified in your ELL's needs analysis.

4. A set of recommendations for your ELL's future language development covering 5 x 45-minute lessons, based on the needs analysis and the result of your one-on-one lesson
5. A bibliography of your research sources

Please note that the ELL you choose must be a genuine language learner. The person cannot be a family member or relative. You are allowed to select your ELL, or you can ask the training course provider to refer one to you.

How to analyse your ELL's needs

Reading

Give your ELL a short reading task to test abilities in one or more reading sub-skills. The text should match your ELL's English level. You can also use article skimming to assess reading longer texts. You need to write up the results showing:

1. the task(s) you set and your ELL's responses
2. a description of your ELL's general first language and English language reading habits
3. any advice you gave your ELL to help develop reading skills

Listening

Give your ELL a short listening task to test intensive listening skills. You can also check and test listening skills during conversations with your ELL. You need to write up the results showing:

1. the task(s) you set and your ELL's responses
2. the conversation with your ELL demonstrating understanding and response
3. your ELL's English language listening habits, e.g. radio, TV, internet, movies, etc.
4. any advice you gave your ELL to help develop listening skills

Speaking

You must perform two sets of speaking analyses covering phonology and grammar.

This section must contain:

1. A written transcript of about one minute of your recorded interview with your ELL. If there are pauses or you have to talk, edit these parts out but explain what you took out and why e.g. [I asked a question here]. The idea is to get a transcript covering roughly one minute of your ELL speaking.
2. You must comment on your ELL's fluency and communication skills
3. Using the one-minute recording used in point 1, you must select one or more segments totalling 20 to 30 words. You must transcribe the words in plain English and as phonemically spoken. You may choose a block of 20 to 30 words or a set of small blocks adding up to 20 to 30 words. If you go for smaller blocks, each block must contain at least five words.

Your phonemic transcription must show error analysis covering:

1. two features of segmental phonology (sound)
2. two features of suprasegmental phonology (e.g. stress, intonation, elision)

Your phonemic transcription should illustrate:

1. That you can apply the phonology knowledge learnt in Unit 2
2. Your listening skills, especially sound discrimination
3. Your ability to spot word stress and intonation
4. Setting your teaching priorities about pronunciation, accuracy, and other teaching objectives

You present your error analysis in a table. You can add a summary as well if you wish. You have to document a minimum of four and a maximum of eight errors.

Example analysis of errors in spoken English

Speaking: Pronunciation analysis				
Number (refers to phonologically transcribed segment(s))	Error	Correction	Orthographic representation	Analysis/reason for error
1	/gret/	/greɪt/	great	Vowel clusters are rare in Turkish, so learners often stumble with vowel clusters. In this case, this caused a stress error, the student used short sound instead of long sound.
7	/ˈkɒligz/	/ˈkɒliːgz/	colleagues	Vowel clusters are rare in Turkish, so learners often stumble with vowel clusters. In this case, this caused a stress error, the student used short sound instead of long sound.

Speaking: Spoken lexis and grammar analysis				
Line (refers to orthographically transcribed passage)	**Type of error**	**Error**	**Correction**	**Analysis**
6	We rented car.	We rented a car.	Indefinite articles	In the student's native language, article usage is not necessary
8	They were also in United States to improve their English.	They were also in the United States to improve their English.	Definite article	In the student's native language, article usage is not necessary
12	I had the chance to get know different accents.	I had the chance to get to know different accents.	Collocations	The student had confused the 'to' usages. Because he had used 'to' between two verbs, he forgot to use 'to' in collocation.

Writing

Get a sample of your ELLs written English for analysis. You can do this either by setting a task or looking at some recent work your ELL may have done in an English class. You need to include the original corrected versions in your portfolio. The results should have line numbers so that you can refer to them. The ELL's written work should be handwritten. For example, you could ask your ELL to write a letter to you or respond to a theme.

Your writing analysis has two parts that focus on:

1. grammar, lexis, spelling and punctuation
2. organisation, register and handwriting

Part A:

1. grammar accuracy: structural analysis of strengths and weaknesses
2. lexical range and accuracy: analyse your ELL's use of written vocabulary
3. spelling
4. punctuation

Part B:

1. How effectively did your ELL communicate meaning?
2. Did your ELL get the right level of formality (register)?
3. Was the text organised in terms of paragraphs and sentence links?
4. Was your ELL's handwriting legible?

You present your results in a table. You can add a summary as well if you wish. You have to document a minimum of four and a maximum of eight errors.

Example analysis of errors in written English

Writing: Grammar and lexis analysis				
Line in the learner's writing	**Error type**	**Error**	**Correction**	**Analysis/reason for error**
3	communication mediums	communication media	Grammatical-Nouns that are singular in form but plural in meaning	In the learner's native language, the plural nouns are less used than in English. In this case, the learner has overstated the plural noun usage and missed the rule for the singular form.
4	on the world	in the world	Grammatical-Prepositions	Prepositions at/in/on cause confusion for Turkish native speakers because the Turkish language doesn't have specific differences in meaning with those propositions.

The one-on-one lesson

The required material for the one-on-one lesson must contain:

1. Your rationale for choosing your lesson objectives

2. Your lesson plan should show correcting written language, discussion of the analysis reading comprehension tasks, build on an identified area of your ELL's language skills that need attention
3. A lesson plan
4. Your post-lesson evaluation and self-reflection should include your reflection about your one-on-one teaching experience compared to teaching a class of students
5. The materials you used in the one-on-one lesson

Recommendations for further study

After you teach your class, you have to write up 5 x 45-minute lesson descriptions designed to continue the one-on-one class you gave to the ELL. Each lesson needs a rationale.

Example table to present recommendations for further study

Lesson	Functional /structural objectives	Skills objectives	Phonological objectives	Lexical objectives	Rationale
1	Vowel and consonant clusters pronunciation	To develop speaking skills to talk at conference calls.	To practise the pronunciation of vowel and consonant clusters	To learn the use of vocabulary and terminology used in conference calls	During conference calls, he needs to use correct and clear pronunciation. He often has conference calls with colleagues from different countries, and they communicate in English.
2	To be able to use correct definite and indefinite articles.	To practise and develop skimming/ scanning reading skills through a text that includes definite and indefinite articles.	To practise the pronunciation of /ð/ sound for the "the"	To learn the use of proper nouns that need to be used with "the" and without "the"	The student had difficulties with definite and indefinite articles, and he needs to learn the correct articles.

Bibliography

Create a bibliography for your references to external sources.

Unit 4 – Materials assignment

The materials assignment tests your ability to plan, produce, use and evaluate basic classroom teaching material based on the material you have used during teaching practice.

You create and use your teaching material in one of your teaching practice classes and then write a rationale and evaluation of the effectiveness of your teaching material.

The final part of **Unit 4 -Materials assignment** is a one-on-one interview with the independent external moderator where you must reflect on and discuss the use of your teaching material.

The independent external moderator gives your **Unit 4 - Materials assignment** grade. To pass Unit 4, you must score at least 14 out of 24 on a graded marking scale.

You do this assignment individually. You can share ideas and experiences with your classmates, but what you create must be your work.

Your course trainer:

1. provides support and guidance
2. tells you about the assessment criteria
3. allows you to rehearse your independent external moderator interview
4. gives you constructive feedback

Unit 4 structure

There are three components (details below):

1. Creating and using your teaching material
2. Writing up your results that reflect on why you created your teaching material and how effective it was
3. A one-on-one interview with the independent external moderator who will review your teaching material, judge your performance and give you your Unit 4 grade

Creating and using your material

The teaching material you use must be linked to one of your teaching practice tasks. You must build it into one of your observed and assessed lesson plans and use it during the lesson.

The teaching material you use must be unique. For example, you cannot re-use teaching material you used in other lessons or your one-on-one class from your **Unit 3 – Learner profile** material.

The use of new material

You can create new teaching material. How you make it is your choice as long as the final product can be used as input for components 2 and 3 listed above.

The use of existing material

You can use existing teaching material, but you must demonstrate imaginative and significant adaptation and use of the existing teaching material. In addition,

you have to show that you have extended the existing teaching material beyond what was initially suggested by the teaching material's guidelines. Finally, if you use existing teaching material, you must cite and acknowledge the source.

We recommend that your choice of existing teaching material should be limited to:

1. any teaching material you have used before that worked well but can be further adapted and improved
2. teaching material that was not a success in a previous lesson but contributed significantly to your ELLs' learning

The written assignment

Your written assignment comprises:

1. Rationale
2. Evaluation

Rationale

Your rationale explains why you developed the teaching material for your ELLs that you thought would help achieve your lesson's objectives.

The rationale must include:

1. Information about your class
2. What you expect to achieve from a linguistics perspective (linguistic aims)
3. Your objectives for your ELLs language development (linguistic aims)
4. What you expect your ELLs to achieve (anticipated achievements)
5. The difficulties that may arise when your ELLs use your teaching material and how you will address them if they arise (anticipated achievements)

Your anticipated linguistic aim is the language area or skill you will work on and how you will deliver. For example, new language, structures, functions, semantics, etc. You must take the learning exercise further than just conversation practice.

Your anticipated achievements cover linguistic issues like your ELLs current knowledge and skills, pronunciation challenges, organising your ELLs in groups, motivation, etc.

Evaluation

The evaluation section explains how you used your teaching material in the classroom and how effective it was. In addition, the evaluation must give reasons for the success (or lack of) of the materials. This section must also explain any improvements for the teaching material for use with identical learners without changing the learning objectives.

Assessment interview

The assessment interview focuses on

1. your rationale and evaluation
2. your ELLs and their needs.

Your assessment covers:

1. the suitability of your teaching material for your ELLs' needs and motivation
2. any problems you had during the lesson
3. how you dealt with the problems
4. how your ELLs responded to your teaching material
5. how you can improve the teaching material for future use
6. An appraisal of:
   a. How you selected and made your teaching material
   b. How you could teach using teaching material from other sources

Your interview with the independent external moderator lasts for 15 minutes. The independent external moderator reads your rationale and evaluation and then spends about 10 minutes asking you questions based on the 24 points shown below in the **Unit 4 assessment criteria** section.

Unit 4 assessment criteria

The table below shows you the 24 points about which the independent external moderator will question you. The 24 points have a light-orange background. You get 1 point for an acceptable answer. You must score at least 14 points to pass Unit 4.

IMPORTANT: Of all five units in the Trinity CertTESOL course, Unit 4 is the one that you are more likely to fail. Make sure that you are well prepared for the Unit 4 interview.

Your course provider should have time scheduled to help you prepare for your Unit 4 interview.

Assessment criteria table from the Trinity CertTESOL syllabus page 24

	Criterion	To obtain a pass, trainees must get 14 out of a possible 24 marks	
	The trainee can:	One mark per criterion	One mark per criterion
Written communication skills	Identify a linguistic purpose and specific objectives	Identification of a linguistic purpose	Identification of specific objectives
	Explain how the materials were appropriate to the ELLs' linguistic needs	Identification of the class needs	Explanation of how the materials met the class needs
	Identify potential difficulties of the materials for the ELLs and solutions for dealing with them	Identification of potential difficulties	Identification of potential solutions
	Discuss effectively how the materials were used in the classroom	Discussion of ELL groupings used	Discussion of the broader context of using the materials in

			the lesson, e.g. stages of the lesson
	Evaluate the success of the materials	Reasons for the success (or not) of the materials	Indication of how the conclusion was reached
	Suggest how the materials might be improved	Suggestion(s) on how the materials might be improved in terms of relevancy to the linguistic needs of the ELLs	Suggestion(s) of how the materials might be improved in terms of their design and presentation
Oral communication skills	Discuss the suitability of the materials both in terms of needs and motivation for the ELLs	Discussion of the suitability of the materials in terms of ELL needs	Discussion of the suitability of the materials in terms of ELL motivation
	Discuss what problems arose from the materials and how these were dealt with	Discussion of the problems that arose	Discussion of the solutions to these problems
	discuss how the ELLs responded to the materials and why you thought this was the case	Discussion of the ELLs' response to the materials	Reason(s) why the learners responded in this way
	Discuss what the learning outcomes were from the materials and how the materials might be improved	Discussion of the learning outcomes	Discussion of the potential improvements to the materials
	Demonstrate what you learnt about the selection and production of English language teaching materials	Discussion of the point(s) made about the selection of materials	Discussion of the point(s) made about the production of materials
	Demonstrate what you learnt about teaching English using materials from different sources	Example(s) of what you learnt	Justification for why using self-generated materials is beneficial

Your interview is recorded. If you do not want to be recorded, you cannot be interviewed, and you will fail Unit 4.

Unit 5 – Unknown language

Unit 5 is possibly the most popular in the course. You get to experience what it is like to be a language learner. You get taught a foreign language using the techniques you learn.

Here are a few examples of the languages you might get taught as the **unknown language**:

1. Polish
2. Norwegian
3. Hebrew
4. Tagalog

You will not hear one word of English during your four hours of unknown language classes. The unknown language is the only language you hear in your unknown language classes.

The purpose of **Unit 5 – Unknown language** is to give you:

1. An awareness of what it is like to learn another language in terms of feelings, emotions, frustrations, challenges, etc.
2. The ability to spot the aims and objectives of the lesson
3. The ability to see if your teacher's methodology, materials and class management techniques met the aims and objectives
4. An awareness of a few of the core features of the unknown language versus English
5. Empathy with the people to whom you will teach English

Structure of the Unknown Language Assignment

You get four hours of classes learning an unknown language. The classes emphasise listening and speaking skills. The unknown languages classes are:

1. Taught in one-hour classes
2. Built for beginner level learners
3. Taught by an experienced teacher
4. Use a communicative teaching style
5. Given during the earlier part of the course

You will see some of the methodologies and approaches you learn in Unit 1 that your unknown language teacher puts into practice. Next, you get to establish and record your feelings, emotions and experiences as a language learner. Finally, you get to see how different methods and techniques result in successful learning.

You write up your experiences in your unknown language journal.

The Unknown Language Journal

You have to write up the following in your unknown language journal for each unknown language class.

1. The lesson's objective in terms of learning grammar, language functions and vocabulary
2. A description of the methods, activities and materials your teacher used

3. Observations about your teacher's class-management style and technique
4. Your reflection about:
    a. the learning experience
    b. your teacher's teaching methods
    c. how the methods suited your and your classmates' learning preferences
    d. your classmate's strengths and weaknesses

You must conclude with a summary of your overall experience and an evaluation of the teaching methods. In addition, the summary must include what you will add to your teaching techniques as a result of your Unit 5 experiences.

You must also include a brief description of some of the contrastive features of English versus the unknown langue language. For example, adjective placement, word gender, the equivalent of the neutral "it" in English, etc.

Assessment of the Unknown Language Journal

You get assessed on the accuracy of your analysis and the reflective nature of the journal. You also get guidance about what to look for in the unknown language lessons and instructions for writing your **Unit 5 - Unknown Language Journal**.

Professional awareness and development

In addition to passing the five Units, you must show an awareness of the following "soft skills":

1. the needs of your classmates and colleagues
2. the value of mutual support and teamwork
3. the need for personal development throughout the course
4. a constructive response to training input and feedback from your trainer(s), classmates and ELLs

Your awareness of these critical points is assessed based on your:

1. willingness to attend when required
2. ability to complete all assignments
3. ability to deliver your assignments to schedule
4. contribution to course activities
5. willingness to respect input from others
6. willingness to respect your ELLs' contributions during your practice classes
7. willingness to respect the admin staff
8. ability and desire to take accept and positively react to performance feedback
9. ability to work with your trainer and classmates to develop a constructive dialogue

Your course provider will consider these soft skills as part of your overall assessment and grade.

You should also develop an awareness of:

1. your need for further professional development (reflection and correction, practice, active participation with colleagues, reading, attending seminars/conferences, and formal training)
2. learners' special educational needs
3. working with your classmates to develop teaching techniques to support learners with learning challenges
4. common resources for teaching jobs
5. easily accessible and reliable means of getting job and employer information

Step 6 - Passing your external moderation

Group interview

You get interviewed as a group. Here are some samples of the questions you may get asked.

Section	Example questions
Course admission procedure	How were you interviewed? Face to face, phone, or online?
	Was the intensity of the course explained to you during the interview?
	Was a handwritten task part of the interview?
	Was your suitability for the course fully explained and established?
	Is there anyone under 18 years old?
	Did any of you drop out of secondary education before you were 18?
	Were you asked about any physical or educational special needs you may have?
Pre-course tasks and reading	What happened between the interview and the start of the course?
	Were you given pre-course work and recommended reading?
	When did you get your pre-course work?
	How clear and accurate was the information about the course and the pre-course work?
	Was there any recommended reading? If so, what was it?
	Was this reading helpful?
	What were the recommended tasks? Were these online?
	Did you get feedback on the pre-course tasks or get the answers?
	How helpful was the task as preparation for the course?
Unit 1 Teaching skills (observation)	Did you get clear instructions, guidance and Pro-forma documents to use?
	Were you told how you would get assessed?
	Did you observe experienced teachers?
	How many hours or classes did you observe?
	What did you do while you were observing?
	How accessible were classes and teachers for observation and discussion?
	What was the total time allocated to the observation of classes?
	How was the observation of experienced teachers work integrated with the other course units?

	How helpful was the observation of experienced teachers in achieving the overall aims of the course?
Unit 1 Teaching skills (Teaching practice)	Did you get clear instructions, guidance and Pro-forma documents to use?
	Were you told how you would get assessed?
	Were you introduced to different models of teaching?
	What is PPP, CLT, ESA?
	What do you understand to be the difference between testing and teaching?
	How many hours did you teach?
	Did you teach at different levels?
	Did you start teaching from the first day?
	How much assistance/guidance did you get with your teaching?
	Did you teach a range of lesson types?
	Did you use course books or devise your lessons?
	What were student numbers like on most days?
	What did you do while others in your teaching practice group were teaching?
	Were you given Pro-forma documents, guidance, templates, suggestions, etc.?
	What types of teaching methods did you learn?
	Did your teaching practice classes have people of a similar ability level?
	How many classes did you teach, and was each class observed by a trainer?
	How long was each class you taught?
	Did all the teaching practice equipment or software work properly?
	Can you tell me about some of your teaching practice experiences on the course?
	How did your trainer(s) observe you?
	Did more than one trainer observed one of your lessons?
	Were all your six-hour classes observed and assessed by a trainer?
	How did you observe each other?
	Did you give peer observation feedback to each other? If you did, was it helpful?
	How did your trainer(s) give you teaching practice feedback?
	How was the teaching practice work integrated with the other course units?
	How valuable was the teaching practice in achieving the overall aims of the course?

Unit 2 Language awareness and skills	Were you shown the Trinity syllabus for Unit 2 - language awareness and skills?
	Were any of the language awareness and skills covered in pre-course reading and the course?
	How were you taught language awareness and skills? For example, reading material, lectures, workshops, online delivery, etc.
	Were you given resources to get more information about language awareness and skills?
	Did you have a language test?
	Was the test run under examination conditions?
	How long was the test?
	How were the language awareness and skills work integrated with the other course units?
	How valuable was the language awareness and skills in achieving the overall aims of the course?
Unit 3 Learner profile	Did you get clear instructions, guidance and Pro-forma documents to use?
	Were you told how you would get assessed?
	How did you find the learner profile?
	How did you find your learner?
	Did you encounter any problems?
	How did you prepare for interviewing, profile writing and teaching your one-to-one class?
	How did you arrange interview time(s) with your learner?
	What did you ensure your learner completed the work?
	Can you tell me some of the inputs that applied to the learner profile?
	How was the learner profile work integrated with the other course units?
	How helpful was the learner profile in achieving the overall aims of the course?
Unit 4 Materials assignment	Did you get clear instructions, guidance and Pro-forma documents to use?
	Were you told how you would get assessed?
	When did you first find out about the materials assignment?
	Were you well-prepared for the materials assignment interview?
	Did you rehearse for today's moderation interview?
	How was the materials assignment work integrated with the other course units?
	How valuable was the materials assignment in achieving the overall aims of the course?

Unit 5 Unknown language	Did you get clear instructions, guidance and Pro-forma documents to use?
	Were you told how you would get assessed?
	How did you find the unknown language element of the course?
	Were there clear guidelines for the assignment?
	What preparation and written guidance did you get for observation and journal writing?
	Was appropriate input provided before starting assignments?
	How was the unknown language work integrated with the other course units?
	How valuable was the unknown language unit in achieving the overall aims of the course?
Tutorials and feedback	Did your input sessions reflect what you experienced in teaching practice?
	How were you given feedback after you taught?
	Was feedback constructive?
	Did it reflect how you felt about your lesson?
	How did you reflect on your teaching?
	Were you told after each lesson whether it was a pass or fail?
	Were you or would you have been warned if lessons were below standard?
	Were your tutorials given at appropriate points in the course?
	Did any of you get a warning about weaker areas or a potential failing grade?
	Were the main points discussed in tutorials confirmed in writing?
Testing and assessment	Did you learn about different language examinations used to test English language levels? Two examples are the IELTS and GESE examinations.
	What types of exams did you cover?
	Did you find this helpful?
Professional awareness and development	What do professional awareness and development mean?
	How were these two concepts presented?
	What do you feel you learned from each other?
	What do you feel you learned from your trainer(s)?
	Did you get advice about jobs, continuing professional and career development?
Timetabling	Were you given clear deadlines for all assignments?
	Was the timetable clear at the start of the course for input, teaching practice and feedback?

	Did your timetable change during the course? If it did, were you informed?
	Was there a sensible and helpful balance of components within the timetable?
Premises, equipment and resources	(Face to face courses only) How did you like the training area in terms of space, cleanliness and quietness?
	(Face to face courses only) Did you have a study area? If you did, was it big enough, clean and quiet?
	(Face to face courses only) How were the general facilities (toilets, washing facilities and refreshments)?
	(Face to face courses only) If any equipment was made available, was it in good working order? Examples: audio equipment, overhead projectors, boards, interactive whiteboards, photocopying facilities
	(Face to face courses only) Was there internet access and computing facilities?
	(Face to face courses only) Were there signs and information about emergency procedures?
Course management and administration	Were you told who your trainer was?
	How efficient was the payment process?
	(Face to face courses only) If you got offered accommodation, was it suitable and value for money?
	How helpful were the administrative staff?
Overall view of the course	What were your expectations of the course, and how far were these met?
	How far was the course as described in the promotional and in-course literature?
	In terms of content and mode of delivery: What were the most valuable aspects of the course? What were the least valuable aspects of the course?
	How helpful was the training staff?
	How would you rate the subject expertise and professionalism of your trainer(s)?
	Did you learn about continuing professional development?
	Do you feel prepared for a first (or next) teaching post?
Summary questions	What recommendations would you suggest to improve the course?
	Would you recommend the course to a friend?

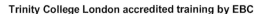

| | Was the course professionally delivered and stimulating? |
| | Was the course value for money? |

Unit 4 interview

Refer to the **Assessment interview** paragraph in the **Unit 4 – Materials assignment** section.

Getting your certificate

At the end of the course, your course provider tells you if you passed or got referred.

If you got referred, read the next section.

If you passed, Trinity College London is immediately informed, and schedule your certificate for printing.

Trinity College London sends your printed certificate to your course provider.

Your course provider contacts you for a mailing address and surfaces mails the CertTESOL certificate to you.

IMPORTANT: Ensure your address is correct and that the certificate is delivered to someone if you are not at home.

Referral – retaking one or more failed units

If you did not make the grade for one or more course units, you get a Referral grade.

A referral is not the end of the road. You can retake the referred units to get a passing grade.

Retaking referred units is agreed upon between you and your training centre. You get rescheduled for the moderation of your new material.

You only get one shot to retake your referred Unit (s), so we strongly recommend doing what it takes to pass the course the first time around.

There is no charge for retaking Unit 4. However, there are charges for retaking the other units. You pay these charges directly to Trinity College.

We repeat, do the right thing and don't get referred.

Appendices

Appendix A – Teaching practice assessment criteria

Appendix B   Terminology and definitions

Appendix C – Bibliography and references

Appendix D – Unit referral procedure

Appendix A – Teaching practice assessment criteria

TEACHING PRACTICE	A	B	C	D	E
Aims: wording & achievement	Clear aims, appropriate to the level, which are fully realised. Fully accurate research of target language (form, meaning, use, pronunciation).	Reasonably clear aims, which are appropriate to level and realised in broad terms. Mostly accurate research of target language (F, M, U, P).	Aims may be slightly inappropriate to level or vague. Inconsistent achievement of aims, but broadly realised. Partially accurate research of target language (F, M, U, P).	Very vague/inappropriate aims that remain largely unfulfilled, little evidence of any effective planning or research of target language (F, M, U, P).	Completely fails to satisfy course requirements.
Rapport / Management	Creates a very friendly, enjoyable atmosphere on both class /individual level. Teacher is fully in control of lesson direction during the class.	A generally friendly/enjoyable atmosphere despite occasional lapses. Teacher largely in control of events and student activity.	Lesson conducted in appropriate manner but lacking warmth and support of A/B grades on either class/ individual level. Teacher maintains appropriate overall control despite some slips.	A sometimes tense atmosphere with trainee failing to respond adequately to class or individuals. Students' activity is not under control too often.	As above.
Professionalism /Preparedness	Fully ready in terms of teaching aids and knowledge of lesson's content & purpose. Appearance is thoroughly professional.	Majority of lesson content is well prepared, but slips may occur. Appears to be largely in control of lesson events.	Overall level of preparation is satisfactory but key elements leave room for improvement.	Trainee does not appear as professional and demonstrates insufficient readiness regarding materials and lesson content.	As above.
Materials	Produces materials of an almost professional standard, fully relevant to the lesson.	Produces materials of high standard, which are generally relevant to lesson objectives.	Materials are of presentable standard, though not always clearly applicable to lesson objectives.	Materials are often unclear or untidy and lacking in relevance to lesson objectives.	As above.
STT/TTT	Keeps TTT to a minimum, providing every opportunity for STT/ real communication.	Keeps TTT low whilst regularly using strategies to encourage STT and real communication.	TTT is sometimes excessive and does not consistently facilitate STT/ real communication.	TTT is excessive and detrimental to student communication. Fails to facilitate opportunities for STT.	As above.
Instruction / Teacher language	Very clear and concise instructions and examples, fully appropriate to learners' level of English.	Instructions/examples clear and concise, appropriate to learners' level of English.	Instructions/explanations are occasionally vague, not concise or inappropriate to learners' level of English.	Instructions/explanations are often confusing, not concise or inappropriate to learners' level of English.	As above.
Interactions, Pace & Timing	Portrays a variety of interaction patterns, fully appropriate to lesson stages. Maintains a lively pace, while reacting to learner needs. Planned timings are accurate.	Utilises a reasonable variety of patterns, generally appropriate to lesson stage. Lesson consistently conducted at reasonable pace with timings well estimated.	Utilises some different interaction patterns, which may not be fully appropriate to lesson stage. Pace occasionally lags & plan suffers.	Little exploitation of different interaction patterns, or patterns used at inappropriate lesson stage. Pace slow/de-motivating. Planned timings are wholly inaccurate.	As above.
Correction	Uses a wide variety of correction techniques in a sympathetic manner in appropriate situations	Demonstrates a variety of correction techniques generally appropriate to situation, in a supportive manner.	Might use a wider variety of techniques. Correction sometimes inappropriate to situation or done in unsympathetic manner.	Little correction taking place or inappropriate techniques being used. Manner of correction is often unsympathetic.	As above.
Feedback	Contributes fully and supportively to sessions, often leading feedback into relevant areas focusing on positive/weaker areas.	Makes regular, relevant contributions to feedback, showing an appreciation of positive/weaker areas.	Contributes to feedback though comments sometimes lack insight or concentrate overly on either strong/weak points.	Fails to show significant appreciation of lesson's effectiveness, or its strong/weak areas.	As above.
Lesson plan/ Self evaluation	Lesson plans always extremely clear and well-presented. Self-evaluations demonstrate deep reflective thinking beyond lesson feedback.	Lesson plans are clear and easy to follow. Self-evaluations show lesson has been carefully considered in detail.	Lesson plans are clearly presented in places. Self-evaluations show some appreciation of lesson outcomes.	Lesson plans are untidy or difficult to follow. Self-evaluations do not really show appreciation of lesson outcomes.	As above.

Appendix B – Terminology and definitions

Action verbs	A verb to express action, for example, "Drive", as in "We often **drive** past their house."
Active voice	The form of a phrase or sentence where the subject is doing something, e.g. "John rode his bicycle."
Adjective	A word that modifies a noun to highlight qualities, quantity or extent, e.g. "That is a **red** car." "There are **five** birds in the tree." "That is a **big** cake." red, five, and big are adjectives.
Adjunct	A word or word group that qualifies or completes the meaning of another word or word group but is not a primary structural element in a sentence, e.g. "I have never met Dave **before**." Before is an adjunct because you could remove it, and the sentence would still be valid.
Adverbial phrase	A group of words performing the task of an adverb, e.g. "Children **grow up** quickly." grow up is an adverbial phrase.
Adverb	A word that sets the scope of verb, adjectives, other adverbs, phrases, and sentences. Adverbs answer when? where? how? how much? how long? or how often? E.g. "He walked **slowly**." "I leave for Spain **tomorrow**." Slowly and tomorrow are adverbs.
Affirmative	A sentence or statement that is positive, e.g. "I am a teacher."
Antonym	Words that mean the opposite of something, e.g. hot - cold, tall - short
Article	A word that describes specific or unspecific nouns and noun equivalents. There are three articles in English 'a', 'an' and 'the'. "The" is referred to as a definite article. "A" and "an" are referred to as indefinite articles, e.g. "I read **the** report." "I will have **an** interview next week."
Auxiliary verb	Aka the "helping verb" it is used with a main verb to help express the main verb's tense, mood, or voice. The main auxiliary verbs are to be, to have, and to do, e.g. "She was **waiting** for an hour.", "The phone has been **disconnected**.", "**Don't forget** your wallet."
Collocation	How words go together or form fixed relationships, e.g. "heavy rain", "high temperature", "winding road".
Comparative	Compares a person or object with another and indicates which has more or less of a certain quality, e.g. "John runs **faster** than Dave."
Complement	Adds information about the subject or the object, e.g. "Sheila is a **nurse**." and "He made me **very angry**." a nurse and very angry are complements.
Conjunction	Connects words, phrases, clauses, or sentences, e.g. and, because, but, neither, so, etc.
Contraction	A shortened version of a word or phrase, e.g. I am = I'm, will = 'll as in I'll, she'll, etc.
Contrastive analysis	The study and comparison of two languages looking at structural similarities and differences. There are two central aims 1) establish the inter-relationships of the languages and 2) to aid second language acquisition.
Coordinate conjunction	Seven words that are used to connect two words. The seven are for, and, nor, but, or, yet, and so. Examples slowly but surely, they ran and jumped, would you like tea or coffee?
Countable noun	A noun that can be counted, e.g. rooms, fingers, shoes as opposed to nouns that cannot be counted, e.g. money, coffee, salt.
Derivation	Creating a new word from a word, usually by adding a prefix or a suffix, e.g. use = usable, infect = disinfect.
Determiner	A word that introduces or precedes a noun, e.g. **three** boys, **the** door. Three and they are determiners.

Direct object	The object directly influenced by the verb in the sentence, e.g. "He is playing **the guitar**." Playing refers to the guitar, so the guitar is the direct object.
Elision	Combining more than one sound into one, e.g. "**do not**" becomes the elision "**don't**"
ELL	English Language Learner.
Extensive listening and reading	Extensive listening and reading are long listening and reading activities and may vary from a few minutes to several hours.
Hyponyms	A subclass of words under a class, e.g. vehicle is a class and bus, car, taxi are subclasses of vehicle. Bus, car and taxi are hyponyms of vehicle.
Indirect object	The secondary object in a sentence that must contain a direct object, e.g. "Jane bought a present for **her friend**." Jane bought a present is a direct object form, so the indirect object is her friend. Alternatively, you could ask "For whom did Jane buy a present?" answer, her friend (the indirect object).
Infinitive verb	A verb prefixed with "to", e.g. to run, to sit.
Inflexions	Letters added to nouns, adjectives, and verbs to show their different grammatical forms, e.g. flower - flowers, run - running, jump - jumped.
Intensive listening and reading	Extensive listening and reading are short listening and reading activities, usually no more than a few minutes.
Interlingual interference	The effect of language forms when two languages cross or overlap, e.g. a beginner level ELL from Spain may write "the tree green" because in Spanish, the adjective follows the noun.
International Phonetic Alphabet (IPA)	An academic standard created by the International Phonetic Association. It is a phonetic notation system using symbols to represent spoken language sounds in all languages spoken on earth.
Interrogative	A sentence or statement that asks a question, e.g. "Are you a teacher?"
L1	A language learner's first language aka mother tongue.
Language acquisition	The process of learning a language.
Language decoding	The mental process of converting what you read into speech i.e. reading and speaking.
Language encoding	The mental process of converting what you hear into text i.e. listening and writing.
Lesson planning	The process of designing and writing a list of tasks and supporting material to be used to teach a class.
Lexis	Another word for vocabulary; the words that make up a language.
Linguistic form	A meaningful unit of speech, e.g. a word or a sentence
Linguistic function	The different ways that language is used, e.g. to converse, to inform, to direct, etc.
Linguistic profile	An analysis of someone's language skills usually to find areas that need improvement.
Main verb	The primary focus of a sentence, e.g. "John **kicked** the ball " To kick is the main verb. There could be more than one if there are conjunctions, e.g. "John **kicked** the ball **and ran** towards the goal." To kick and to run are main verbs.
Modal auxiliary verbs	Modal auxiliary verbs (aka modal verbs and modals) are used to change the meaning of other verbs by expressing modality, i.e. asserting or denying possibility, likelihood, ability, permission, obligation, or future intention, e.g. "I **might** go to Paris tomorrow."
Needs analysis	An analysis of the learning needs of one or more learners.
Negative	A sentence or statement that is negative, e.g. "I am **not** a teacher."

Noun phrases	Combined words that act like a noun and can be replaced by a pronoun, e.g. "**This sentence** contains **two noun phrases**." – "**It** contains **them**." "**The subject noun phrase that is present in this sentence** is long." – "**It** is long." – "**Noun phrases** can be embedded in **other noun phrases**." – "**They** can be embedded in **them**."
Nouns	Words representing a specific object or set of objects, such as living creatures, places, actions, qualities, states of existence, or ideas.
Object	See Direct and Indirect objects.
Orthographic transcription	The conversion of the spoken word to text using standard spelling and punctuation conventions.
Paralinguistic devices	Non-language expressions e.g. body language, gestures, facial expressions, tone and pitch of voice.
Passive voice	A language construct where the subject of the verb is the recipient (not the source) of the action denoted by the verb, e.g. "The ball was kicked by John." is passive, John kicked the ball is active.
Phoneme	The smallest phonetic unit in a language that is capable of conveying a distinction in meaning e.g. the letter **m** in **mat**.
Phonemic symbols	Symbols that represent individual phoneme sounds, e.g. /p/ in **p**et and /ei/ as in p**ay**.
Phonemic transcription	A system used for writing down sounds in speech using letters or symbols usually taken from the IPA.
Phonics	A method of teaching elementary reading and spelling based on the phonetic interpretation of ordinary spelling.
Phonology	The study of language speech sounds with reference to their distribution and patterning and to rules governing pronunciation.
Phrasal verbs	Verbs comprising more than one word, e.g. to take off, to throw out, to put in, etc.
Predicate	The part of a sentence that tells you what the subject did, e.g. "Dave **rode his bicycle**." - rode his bicycle is the predicate.
Prepositional phrase	A group of words consisting of a preposition, its object, and any words that modify the object, e.g. "He arrived **on time**.", "Is she really going out **with him**?"
Prepositions	Usually a common word showing direction, location, time, or that introduces an object that is usually followed by an object. Common prepositions are at, by, for, from, in, of, on, to, and with. Other common prepositions are about, above, across, after, against, along, among, around, because of, before, behind, below, beneath, beside, between, close to, down, during, except, inside, instead of, into, like, near, off, on top of, onto, out of, outside, over, past, since, through, toward, under, until, up, upon, within, without.
Productive skills	Collective term for speaking and writing.
Pronoun	A word that substitutes for a noun or noun phrase, e.g. he, she, it, them, they.
Quantifier	Indicates the quantity of an object e.g. **five** people, **ten** fingers, **a lot of** money, **plenty** of food.
Rationale	A rational explanation or statement of reasons for doing something that answers a question like "Why did you do it?"
Receptive skills	Collective term for listening and reading.
Reported speech	A form of speech that expresses what someone said, but does not use the person's actual words, e.g. "Your partner **said** you don't like tripe.", "The customers **complained** about the person who was smoking."
Scanning	Reading a text to find specific information, e.g. figures, dates or names.

Segmental phonology	See phoneme.
Skimming	Reading a text quickly to get a general idea of meaning.
Stative verb	Expresses a state usually related to thoughts, emotions, relationships, senses, states of being, and measurements, e.g. believe, like, disagree, need, promise, understand.
Strong form	Describes words in a sentence that are stressed or emphasised when spoken.
Subject	The part of a sentence or clause that indicates a) what it is about, or b) who or what performs the action, e.g. "**John** kicked the ball." - John is the subject, "**The report** is accurate." - The report id the subject.
Subordinate conjunctions	Create a link to show cause and effect or time and place relationships, e.g. "He was injured **because** he did not wear a seatbelt.", "**After** I found the key, I opened the door."
Superlative	Expresses that someone or something is at the top of its class, e.g. "He is the **tallest** in his family.", "That is the **fastest** car in the world."
Suprasegmental phonology	Intonation patterns, stress placement and rhythm in spoken language.
Synonyms	Different words that have equivalence, e.g. synonym = equivalent, hot = tropical
Syntactical elements	Words, phrases, sentences and other elements associated with created well-formed language statements.
Syntax	The study of rules for the formation of grammatical sentences in a language and the study of patterns to form sentences and phrases from words.
Tenses	Indicates when the action in a sentence is happening, e.g. "I ran last week." – past. "I will run next week." – future. "I am watching the television." – present.
Verb	A language component that expresses existence, action, or occurrence.
Verb phrase	A verb phrase has a main verb alone, or a main verb plus a modal and/or auxiliary verbs. The main verb always comes last. "Your house **is** beautiful.", "You **may have met** him before."
Weak form	Describes words in a sentence that are not stressed or emphasised when spoken.

Appendix C – Bibliography and references

Author	Title	Publisher	Link
Trinity College London (2016)	Trinity College CertTESOL Syllabus	Trinity College London	https://www.trinitycollege.com/resource/?id=5407
Trinity College London (2016)	Certificate in Teaching English to Speakers of Other Languages (CertTESOL) Validation Requirements	Trinity College London	https://www.trinitycollege.com/resource/?id=5365
EBC (2018)	EBC Trinity CertTESOL course	EBC	Internal, not for publication
EBC (2018)	EBC course management and operating policies and procedures	EBC	Internal, not for publication

Appendix D – Unit referral procedure

Step	Details
1	Trainees are referred at the end of the course moderation.
	A trainee can only be referred once and on no more than two internally assessed units (and/or Unit 4 Materials Assignment).
2	The moderator writes in their report:
	<ul><li>who got referred</li><li>which units</li><li>why they were referred</li></ul>
	For Unit 4, the moderator takes a copy of the written rationale and forwards it to Trinity.
3	The course provider marks the internally assessed referred work.
	The deadline for trainees to complete their work is two weeks after the moderation. After that, the trainers have two weeks to mark the assignments and send them to Trinity.
	The course provider and Trinity agree on the dates. The moderator is not involved.
4	The course provider sends the work to Trinity
	For Unit 1: Teaching Skills for each referred lesson the course provider sends:
	<ul><li>the lesson plan</li><li>trainee reflections</li><li>tutor feedback</li><li>assessment criteria</li></ul>
	For Unit 2: Language Awareness, the course provider sends:
	<ul><li>re-submitted test/assignment with marker's comments</li><li>assessment criteria</li></ul>
	For Unit 3: Learner Profile, the course provider sends:
	<ul><li>original assignment with marker's comments</li><li>the re-submitted work written by the trainee, not the materials that were used in the lesson</li><li>tutor feedback</li><li>assessment criteria</li></ul>
	For Unit 5: Unknown Language, the course provider sends:
	<ol><li>original assignment with marker's comments</li><li>the re-submitted work written by the trainee</li><li>tutor feedback</li><li>assessment criteria</li></ol>
	For Unit 4 Materials Assignment, the candidate:
	<ul><li>has another face-to-face assessment</li><li>is assessed for the whole of Unit 4</li></ul>
	Please contact Trinity to organise a re-assessment.

5	If charges are dues, Trinity gets paid by the trainee.
6	Referrals are moderated. The moderations will be every two weeks.
7	The course provider gets the result which can take up to 21 days from the referral submission date.
8	Certificate is sent to the course provider if the candidate is successful. This will take up to four weeks from the time the course provider is informed of the result.

Unit 1 document example

Teaching Practice and Observation Journal

Course

- Trinity College London CertTESOL
- Madrid, Spain / Online Live Streaming
- From [course start date] to [course end date]

Your name

[Put your name here]

Your final reflective statement

Write your self-assessment of your entire teaching practice experience.

NOTE: The template used for lesson plans is *U1_Lesson_Plan_Template*

Lesson 6

Lesson plan

[Insert plan here]

Self-evaluation

[Copy and paste the "**Self-assessment**" section from your lesson plan here]

Trainer evaluation

[Insert your copy of the trainer's feedback for this lesson here]

Lesson materials

[Insert the materials you used in this lesson here]

Lesson 5

Lesson plan

[Insert plan here]

Self-evaluation

[Copy and paste the "**Self-assessment**" section from your lesson plan here]

Trainer evaluation

[Insert your copy of the trainer's feedback for this lesson here]

Lesson materials

[Insert the materials you used in this lesson here]

Lesson 4

Lesson plan

[Insert plan here]

Self-evaluation

[Copy and paste the "**Self-assessment**" section from your lesson plan here]

Trainer evaluation

[Insert your copy of the trainer's feedback for this lesson here]

Lesson materials

[Insert the materials you used in this lesson here]

Lesson 3

Lesson plan

[Insert plan here]

Self-evaluation

[Copy and paste the "**Self-assessment**" section from your lesson plan here]

Trainer evaluation

[Insert your copy of the trainer's feedback for this lesson here]

Lesson materials

[Insert the materials you used in this lesson here]

Lesson 2

Lesson plan

[Insert plan here]

Self-evaluation

[Copy and paste the "**Self-assessment**" section from your lesson plan here]

Trainer evaluation

[Insert your copy of the trainer's feedback for this lesson here]

Lesson materials

[Insert the materials you used in this lesson here]

Lesson 1

Lesson plan

[Insert plan here]

Self-evaluation

[Copy and paste the "**Self-assessment**" section from your lesson plan here]

Trainer evaluation

[Insert your copy of the trainer's feedback for this lesson here]

Lesson materials

[Insert the materials you used in this lesson here]

Guided observation section

Note: The template used is ***U1d_Observation_Template***

Guided Observation of an experienced teacher's class 1

[Insert your completed observation template for class 1]

Guided Observation of an experienced teacher's class 2

[Insert your completed observation template for class 2]

Guided Observation of an experienced teacher's class 3

[Insert your completed observation template for class 3]

[Insert your completed observation template for class 4]

Peer observation section

Note: The template used is *U1d_Peer_Observation_Template*

Observation for a peer's teaching practice class 1

[Insert your completed observation template for a peer's TP class 1]

Observation for a peer's teaching practice class 2

[Insert your completed observation template for a peer's TP class 1]

Observation templates

Guided Observation Class 1

Your name	
Date	**DD/MM/YYYY**
Level	**Beginner / Intermediate / Advanced**
Group description	
Lesson duration	
Teacher's aim	
What to look for	<ul><li>Describe the teacher's rapport with the class as a whole.</li><li>Comment on the teacher language, specifically instructions and explanations</li></ul>
Your comments	<ul><li>Which aspects do you feel most confident about replicating in your lessons?</li><li>Which aspects do you still think you will struggle with and why?</li><li>What did you learn from the lesson with relevance to your teaching?</li></ul>

Guided Observation Class 2

Your name	
Date	**DD/MM/YYYY**
Level	**Beginner / Intermediate / Advanced**
Group description	
Lesson duration	
Teacher's aim	
What to look for	• How well did the teacher use resources (incl. the board)? • What visuals, videos, variety of resources and language skills, etc., were used? • Did the resources engage the students?
Your comments	• Which aspects do you feel most confident about replicating in your lessons? • Which aspects do you still think you will struggle with and why? • What did you learn from the lesson with relevance to your teaching?

Guided Observation Class 3

Your name	
Date	**DD/MM/YYYY**
Level	**Beginner / Intermediate / Advanced**
Group description	
Lesson duration	
Teacher's aim	
What to look for	• What was the balance of STT (Student Talking Time) and TTT (Teacher Talking Time)? • How did the teacher monitor progress and provide feedback? • How did the students react to the feedback?
Your comments	• Which aspects do you feel most confident about replicating in your lessons? • Which aspects do you still think you will struggle with and why? • What did you learn from the lesson with relevance to your teaching?

Guided Observation Class 4

Your name	
Date	**DD/MM/YYYY**
Level	**Beginner / Intermediate / Advanced**
Group description	
Lesson duration	
Teacher's aim	
What to look for	• Was the lesson coherent? • Did it flow smoothly using appropriate transitions? • How was the integration of vocabulary and grammar? • Was use made of context clues and hints to help the students?
Your comments	• Which aspects do you feel most confident about replicating in your lessons? • Which aspects do you still think you will struggle with and why? • What did you learn from the lesson with relevance to your teaching?

Peer observation template

Your name	
Date	**DD/MM/YYYY**
Level	**Beginner / Intermediate / Advanced**
Group description	
Lesson duration	
Teacher's aim	
Teacher's rapport	• Describe the teacher's rapport with the class as a whole. • Describe the teacher's interaction with individual learners. • Detail the teacher's physical position and movement.
Teacher's delivery	• Describe the speed, clarity and volume of the teacher's voice. • Was the teacher's language graded appropriately to the students' ability level? • Describe how the teacher gave instructions? • How clear were the feedback sessions? How did the teacher use the board to help? • What use was made of gestures and facial signals? • What was the ratio of teacher talking time (TTT) versus student talking time (STT)?
Your comments	• Which aspects do you feel most confident about replicating in your first lesson? • Which aspects do you still think you will struggle with and why? • What did you learn from the lesson with relevance to your teaching?

Unit 3 document example

Learner Profile Section 1: Learner Biography

Your Name	
ELL	**Only put the ELL's first name**
Biographical Details	Refer to student background, e.g. previous learning experiences; how learner uses English now; why learner needs English now and likely use of it in future. (approx. 400 words)
Question list	A list of questions for the speaking and listening analysis
Background	What are some of the main linguistic features of your learner's mother tongue? Refer to one or two areas of grammar, vocabulary, pronunciation. (approx. 300 words).

Learner Profile Section 2: Reading and Listening Skills

Your Name	
ELL	**Only put the ELL's first name**
Reading	Attach a copy of the reading text and accompanying task(s) behind this section.
Tasks	Describe the task set and the learner response to it. What sub-skills were required? E.g. Skimming, Scanning, and Reading for detailed understanding. (approx. 200 words)
ELL's reading habits in English and native language	What kind of reading does the learner do in their L1 and in English? (approx. 100 words)
Advice	What advice can you give the learner to improve to develop their Reading Skill further? (approx. 100 words)
Listening	Attach a copy of the listening task(s) behind this section. You do not need to include the original audio file or the script.
Tasks	Describe the intensive listening task set and the learner response to it. What sub-skills (e.g. listening for gist, specific information, detail) were required? (approx. 200 words)
Voice adjustment	Did you need to rephrase questions or speak unnaturally slowly? (approx. 100 words)

ELL's listening habits in English	What are the learner's general listening habits (in English)? Is the student able to broadly understand, e.g. radio/TV, native speaker conversations? (approx. 100 words)
Advice	What advice can you give the learner to improve? (approx. 100 words)

Learner Profile Section 3: Speaking Skills

Your Name	
ELL	Only put the ELL's first name
ELL fluency	Comment on the learner's fluency and how well they communicated their message in the interview (approx. 200 words). You may refer to overall fluency & effectiveness of communication, range & (briefly) accuracy of vocabulary /grammar. You also can reference elements like hesitation/speed, appropriacy of stress/intonation, etc.
Spoken lexis and grammar analysis	Complete the following table with between 4 and 8 (add extra rows if necessary) errors made by your learner during the needs analysis interview. An example is provided.

Sentence containing error (write out in full so you can show context)	Correction of error	Type of error (use correct terminology here – use a grammar book and refer back to training sessions on error correction)	Analysis/Reason for error
He is the goodest Dad in the world...	...the best Dad...	Grammatical – Superlative adjective	Student has over-applied the rule that superlatives are formed by adding -est onto the adjective. 'Good' is irregular, and so becomes 'best'.
1.			
2.			

3.				
4.				

Transcription	Orthographically transcribe (using standard written English) a segment of at least 20-30 words or several multi-word items together totalling 20-30 words. Number each item/line. An example is provided.
	The purpose of this is to provide you with content from which you can identify pronunciation errors in the learner's speech. So make sure the section you choose contains some pronunciation errors! Specifically, you will need to show a minimum of:
	<ul><li>Two errors of segmental phonology (errors with individual/specific sounds)</li><li>Two errors of suprasegmental phonology (stress, intonation, features of connected speech like elision, intrusion etc.)</li></ul>
	e.g. "1. I love the coffee."
Phonemical transcription 1	Using phonemes, transcribe what you have just written, **as spoken by the ELL**. Underline where errors have been made. Number each item/line*. An example has been provided. /aɪ laːf diː kæfiː/ e.g. 1. ("I love the coffee.")
Phonemical transcription 2	Using phonemes, transcribe the identical phrase **as spoken by a native English speaker**. An example has been provided. /aɪ lʌv ðə kɒfiː/ e.g. 1. ("I love the coffee.")
Pronunciation analysis	Complete the following table with 2 segmental and 2 suprasegmental phonology errors made by your ELL. Two examples are provided.

Transcription line number	Error	Correction	Orthographic representation	Analysis/Reason for error
3	/bæk/	/pæk/	pack	There is no equivalent to the /p/ sound in Arabic (Smith & Swan 2001). The /b/ sound is usually chosen to

				replace it, as Khalid demonstrates here.
5	/ɒv/ /əv/		of	Khalid has not used the weak form for 'of' in this sentence. Foreign students have trouble with identifying and pronouncing weak forms, which have not been formally introduced to Khalid in class.

Learner Profile Section 4: Writing Skills

Your Name	
ELL	**Only put the ELL's first name**
Tasks	Describe the task you will set to measure the ELL's writing skills. (approx. 100 words). Attach the task instructions.
Overall evaluation	Your evaluation of the ELL's writing task in terms of organisation of ideas, communication of meaning, level of formality, punctuation, paragraphing and handwriting. (approx. 200 words) Correct the writing task. Number each line. Attach an unmarked copy and a marked copy of it at the end of this section.
Grammar, Lexis, Spelling and Punctuation	Evaluate the learner's writing task in terms of the following (approx. 200 words in total): 1. Assess the grammatical strengths and weaknesses of the text (make broad generalisations here – do not analyse specific examples) 2. Assess the use of lexis in terms of variety and accuracy 3. Assess the learner's spelling and punctuation
Written Grammar and Lexis analysis	Complete the following table with between 4 and 8 (add extra rows if necessary) errors made by your learner during the needs analysis interview. At least 2 of these

	errors should be (different) examples mentioned in your answer to Q2 A, B or C above. *An example is provided.*

Sentence containing error (write out in full so you can show context)	Correction of error	Type of error (use correct terminology here – use a grammar book and refer back to training sessions on error correction)	Analysis/Reason for error
You must speak it to him.	I am studying	Grammatical – Verb form	Likely to be L1 interference; there is no auxiliary 'be' in Arabic.
1.			
2.			
3.			
4.			

Learner Profile Section 5: The Lesson

You will now teach a lesson of 45 minutes to your ELL using the 1 to 1 lesson plan you wrote.

Learner profile Section 6: Recommendations for further study

Your Name	
ELL	Only put the ELL's first name
Rationale	What is the purpose of each of the 5 recommendations? (approx.. 100 words)
5 recommendations	Complete the table on the next page titled **Recommendations for further study**. Below is an example containing two lesson outlines. Each recommendation must represent high-level content for a 45-minute lesson. Be realistic.

Example recommendations for further study

Lesson	Functional / structural objectives	Skills objectives	Phonological objectives	Lexical objectives	Rationale
1	To be able to use the past.	To develop speaking	To practise the	To learn the use of travel-	The learner was unable to use the

	To talk about the past. To develop the use of simple past tense (regular and irregular verbs).	skills to discuss past travel. To develop the following writing skills: use of past simple to write a postcard describing a journey.	pronunciation of 'ed' endings /t/, /d/, /id/.	related verbs (visited/stayed / travelled/flew/ went, etc).	past tense to talk about her journey to the UK. However, the learner loves travelling and uses English mainly for talking to her friends on topics such as past experiences.
2	To be able to describe regular and current actions. To develop the use of simple present tense and present continuous tense.	To practise and develop skimming/ scanning reading skills.	Not a core focus. Attend to learner need as appropriate.	To learn the use of vocabulary related to domestic routine; collocation of nouns and verbs (make the bed, do the washing, etc).	Habiba had difficulties differentiating between these two structures in use. Needs practice in skimming and scanning to assist her in exam work. Currently reads very slowly.

Recommendations for further study

Lesson	Functional / structural objectives	Skills objectives	Phonological objectives	Lexical objectives	Rationale
1					
2					
3					
4					
5					

Bibliography

You have now completed the Learner Profile Journal.

Add a bibliography including references (published or online) to any sources you used in analysing the typical features of the learner's native language or in planning/teaching the lesson.

Unit 4 document example

TRINITY
COLLEGE LONDON

Unit 4: Materials
Assignment — Pro forma for
trainees' use

Name of trainee: ....

Form 8

Course providing organisation:
Start and end dates of course:

Please complete the summary of class data table below, and all the other information related to the rationale and evaluation sections. Please complete this information in the spaces provided, ensuring that your responses are clearly separated from the rubric.

Please type your answers into the spaces. Clear and coherent notes (e.g. using bullet points) are welcomed, but do not alter the rubric in any way.

The rationale and evaluation have an indicative word count of 500 words in length, excluding the rubric.

Number of learners:	
Level of class:	
Monolingual class (if so, please state first language):	
Type of material:	
Type of activity:	
Point in lesson when used, noting preceding and subsequent activity:	

Rationale and Evaluation

Please show your word count for the rationale and the evaluation, excluding the Trinity rubric. The word count for the rubric is 143 words.

Word count: ....

Rationale

What was the linguistic purpose of this material? What were the objectives for the learners' language development?

How did you think this material was appropriate to your students' specific linguistic needs? Why was it appropriate?

After you had prepared the material and before the lesson, what difficulties did you anticipate for your learners? What solutions did you identify for dealing with those difficulties?

 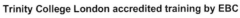
Evaluation

Explain how you used the materials in the classroom effectively. What groupings did you use and why? How did the materials fit within the wider context of the lesson?

What reasons can you give for the success of your materials (or lack of)? How did you reach this conclusion?

How might the materials be improved for the same learners without changing the learning objectives, in terms of targeting the linguistic need and in terms of design and presentation?

Your material

[INSERT YOUR MATERIAL HERE]

Unit 5 document example

UFL Journal lesson notes template – lesson 1

For use after attending each foreign language class

Your Name	
Background	
Date and time	The date and time of the class
Language learned	Name of the language
Number of learners	Total class attendees
Teaching aids	A list of teaching aids used to deliver the class
Lesson purpose	1. Was there a grammar aim? (give examples) 2. Was there a lexical aim? (give examples) 3. Was there a functional aim? (give examples)
Teacher	Keep this section to a maximum of 600 words
Class rapport	Describe your experience
Methods of conveying meaning	Describe your experience
Methods of giving instructions	Describe your experience
Methods of correction	Describe your experience
Encouragement of equal participation	Describe your experience
The proportion of Teacher Talking Time (TTT) and what it consisted of	Describe your experience
Memorable experience	Speak to one of your fellow trainees. What was most memorable (e.g. a piece of language, technique etc.) about the teaching experience?
Peer comments	Comment on your classmates' strengths and needs.
Adoption points	Practical points relevant to your teaching that you will try to adopt (4 bullet points)

Contrastive Language Analysis – lesson 1

Speak with your classmates and contrast any differences or similarities you noticed between the unknown language and English.

Your Name	
Language learned	Name of the language
Grammar	Compare a minimum of 2 aspects between English and the language learned.
Phonology	Compare a minimum of 2 aspects between English and the language learned.
Lexis	Compare a minimum of 2 aspects between English and the language learned.

UFL Journal lesson notes template – lesson 2

For use after attending each foreign language class

Your Name	
Background	
Date and time	The date and time of the class
Language learned	Name of the language
Number of learners	Total class attendees
Teaching aids	A list of teaching aids used to deliver the class
Lesson purpose	1. Was there a grammar aim? (give examples) 2. Was there a lexical aim? (give examples) 3. Was there a functional aim? (give examples)
Teacher	Keep this section to a maximum of 600 words
Class rapport	Describe your experience
Methods of conveying meaning	Describe your experience
Methods of giving instructions	Describe your experience
Methods of correction	Describe your experience
Encouragement of equal participation	Describe your experience
The proportion of Teacher Talking Time (TTT) and what it consisted of	Describe your experience
Memorable experience	Speak to one of your fellow trainees. What was most memorable (e.g. a piece of language, technique etc.) about the teaching experience?
Peer comments	Comment on your classmates' strengths and needs.
Adoption points	Practical points relevant to your teaching that you will try to adopt (4 bullet points)

Contrastive Language Analysis – lesson 2

Speak with your classmates and contrast any differences or similarities you noticed between the unknown language and English.

Your Name	
Language learned	Name of the language
Grammar	Compare a minimum of 2 aspects between English and the language learned.
Phonology	Compare a minimum of 2 aspects between English and the language learned.
Lexis	Compare a minimum of 2 aspects between English and the language learned.

UFL Journal lesson notes template – lesson 3

For use after attending each foreign language class

Your Name	
Background	
Date and time	The date and time of the class
Language learned	Name of the language
Number of learners	Total class attendees
Teaching aids	A list of teaching aids used to deliver the class
Lesson purpose	1. Was there a grammar aim? (give examples) 2. Was there a lexical aim? (give examples) 3. Was there a functional aim? (give examples)
Teacher	Keep this section to a maximum of 600 words
Class rapport	Describe your experience
Methods of conveying meaning	Describe your experience
Methods of giving instructions	Describe your experience
Methods of correction	Describe your experience
Encouragement of equal participation	Describe your experience
The proportion of Teacher Talking Time (TTT) and what it consisted of	Describe your experience
Memorable experience	Speak to one of your fellow trainees. What was most memorable (e.g. a piece of language, technique etc.) about the teaching experience?
Peer comments	Comment on your classmates' strengths and needs.
Adoption points	Practical points relevant to your teaching that you will try to adopt (4 bullet points)

Contrastive Language Analysis – lesson 3

Speak with your classmates and contrast any differences or similarities you noticed between the unknown language and English.

Your Name	
Language learned	Name of the language
Grammar	Compare a minimum of 2 aspects between English and the language learned.
Phonology	Compare a minimum of 2 aspects between English and the language learned.
Lexis	Compare a minimum of 2 aspects between English and the language learned.

UFL Journal lesson notes template – lesson 4

For use after attending each foreign language class

Your Name	
Background	
Date and time	The date and time of the class
Language learned	Name of the language
Number of learners	Total class attendees
Teaching aids	A list of teaching aids used to deliver the class
Lesson purpose	1. Was there a grammar aim? (give examples) 2. Was there a lexical aim? (give examples) 3. Was there a functional aim? (give examples)
Teacher	Keep this section to a maximum of 600 words
Class rapport	Describe your experience
Methods of conveying meaning	Describe your experience
Methods of giving instructions	Describe your experience
Methods of correction	Describe your experience
Encouragement of equal participation	Describe your experience
The proportion of Teacher Talking Time (TTT) and what it consisted of	Describe your experience
Memorable experience	Speak to one of your fellow trainees. What was most memorable (e.g. a piece of language, technique etc.) about the teaching experience?
Peer comments	Comment on your classmates' strengths and needs.
Adoption points	Practical points relevant to your teaching that you will try to adopt (4 bullet points)

Contrastive Language Analysis – lesson 4

Speak with your classmates and contrast any differences or similarities you noticed between the unknown language and English.

Your Name	
Language learned	Name of the language
Grammar	Compare a minimum of 2 aspects between English and the language learned.
Phonology	Compare a minimum of 2 aspects between English and the language learned.
Lexis	Compare a minimum of 2 aspects between English and the language learned.

Summary

Your Name	
Language learned	Name of the language
Summary	Taking all foreign language classes into account, summarise your learning experience as a whole. Evaluate your opinion of this component of the course and the effectiveness or drawbacks of the methodology used, and the learning which took place. Use appropriate terminology where possible and try to develop your ideas beyond mere personal feelings. Think especially about what aspects of the lessons you will utilise when teaching in future. (minimum 500 words)

Printed in Great Britain
by Amazon

36818410R00046